D0947576

That Time

SAMUEL BECKETT

THAT TIME

FABER AND FABER
3 Queen Square
London

First published in 1976
by Faber and Faber Limited
3 Queen Square London WC1
Reprinted 1976
Printed in Great Britain by
Latimer Trend & Company Ltd Plymouth
All rights reserved

ISBN 0 571 11032 0

All applications for performing rights
in *That Time* should be addressed to
Spokesmen, 1 Craven Hill, London, W2

That Time was first performed at the
Royal Court Theatre in the spring of
1976 during a season mounted to mark
the author's seventieth birthday

NOTE

Moments of one and the same voice A B C relay one another
without solution of continuity—apart from the two 10-second
breaks. Yet the switch from one to another must be clearly faintly
perceptible. If threefold source and context prove insufficient
to produce this effect it should be assisted mechanically (e.g.
threefold pitch).

Curtain. Stage in darkness. Fade up to Listener's face about ten feet above stage level midstage off centre.
Old white face, long flaring white hair as if seen from above out-spread.
Voices A B C are his own coming to him from both sides and above. They modulate back and forth without any break in general flow except where silence indicated. See note.
Silence 7 seconds. Listener's eyes are open. His breath audible, slow and regular.

A: that time you went back that last time to look was the ruin
   still there where you hid as a child when was that (*eyes
   close*) grey day took the eleven to the end of the line and
   on from there no no trams then all gone long ago that time
   you went back to look was the ruin still there where you hid
   as a child that last time not a tram left in the place only the
   old rails when was that

C: when you went in out of the rain always winter then always
   raining that time in the Portrait Gallery in off the street out
   of the cold and rain slipped in when no one was looking and
   through the rooms shivering and dripping till you found a
   seat marble slab and sat down to rest and dry off and on to
   hell out of there when was that

B: on the stone together in the sun on the stone at the edge of
   the little wood and as far as eye could see the wheat turning
   yellow vowing every now and then you loved each other just
   a murmur not touching or anything of that nature you one
   end of the stone she the other long low stone like millstone

9

no looks just there together on the stone in the sun with the
little wood behind gazing at the wheat or eyes closed all
still no sign of life not a soul abroad no sound

A: straight off the ferry and up with the nightbag to the high
street neither right nor left not a curse for the old scenes the
old names straight up the rise from the wharf to the high
street and there not a wire to be seen only the old rails all
rust when was that was your mother ah for God's sake all
gone long ago that time you went back that last time to look
was the ruin still there where you hid as a child someone's
folly

C: was your mother ah for God's sake all gone long ago all dust
the lot you the last huddled up on the slab in the old
green greatcoat with your arms round you whose else
hugging you for a bit of warmth to dry off and on to hell
out of there and on to the next not a living soul in the place
only yourself and the odd attendant drowsing around in his
felt shufflers not a sound to be heard only every now and
then a shuffle of felt drawing near then dying away

B: all still just the leaves and ears and you too still on the stone
in a daze no sound not a word only every now and then to
vow you loved each other just a murmur one thing could
ever bring tears till they dried up altogether that thought
when it came up among the others floated up that scene

A: Foley was it Foley's Folly bit of a tower still standing all the
rest rubble and nettles where did you sleep no friend all the
homes gone was it that kip on the front where you no she
was with you then still with you then just the one night in
any case off the ferry one morning and back on her the next
to look was the ruin still there where none ever came where
you hid as a child slip off when no one was looking and
hide there all day long on a stone among the nettles with
your picture-book

C: till you hoisted your head and there before your eyes when
they opened a vast oil black with age and dirt someone

famous in his time some famous man or woman or even
child such as a young prince or princess some young prince
or princess of the blood black with age behind the glass
where gradually as you peered trying to make it out
gradually of all things a face appeared had you swivel on the
slab to see who it was was there at your elbow

B: on the stone in the sun gazing at the wheat or the sky or the
eyes closed nothing to be seen but the wheat turning yellow
and the blue sky vowing every now and then you loved each
other just a murmur tears without fail till they dried up
altogether suddenly there in whatever thoughts you might
be having whatever scenes perhaps way back in childhood
or the womb worst of all or that old Chinaman long before
Christ born with long white hair

C: never the same after that never quite the same but that was
nothing new if it wasn't this it was that common occurrence
something you could never be the same after crawling about
year after year sunk in your lifelong mess muttering to
yourself who else you'll never be the same after this you
were never the same after that

A: or talking to yourself who else out loud imaginary conversa-
tions there was childhood for you ten or eleven on a stone
among the giant nettles making it up now one voice now
another till you were hoarse and they all sounded the same
well on into the night some moods in the black dark or
moonlight and they all out on the roads looking for you

B: or by the window in the dark harking to the owl not a
thought in your head till hard to believe harder and harder
to believe you ever told anyone you loved them or anyone
you till just one of those things you kept making up to keep
the void out just another of those old tales to keep the void
from pouring in on top of you the shroud
(*Silence 10 seconds. Breath audible. After 3 seconds eyes open.*)

C: never the same but the same as what for God's sake did you
ever say I to yourself in your life come on now (*eyes close*)
could you ever say I to yourself in your life turning-point

that was a great word with you before they dried up
altogether always having turning-points and never but the
one the first and last that time curled up worm in slime
when they lugged you out and wiped you off and straightened
you up never another after that never looked back after that
was that the time or was that another time

B: muttering that time together on the stone in the sun or that
time together on the towpath or that time together in the
sand that time that time making it up from there as best you
could always together somewhere in the sun on the towpath
facing downstream into the sun sinking and the bits of
flotsam coming from behind and drifting on or caught in the
reeds the dead rat it looked like came on you from behind
and went drifting on till you could see it no more

A: that time you went back to look was the ruin still there
where you hid as a child that last time straight off the ferry
and up the rise to the high street to catch the eleven neither
right nor left only one thought in your head not a curse for
the old scenes the old names just head down press on up the
rise to the top and there stood waiting with the nightbag
till the truth began to dawn

C: when you started not knowing who you were from Adam
trying how that would work for a change not knowing who
you were from Adam no notion who it was saying what you
were saying whose skull you were clapped up in whose
moan had you the way you were was that the time or was
that another time there alone with the portraits of the dead
black with dirt and antiquity and the dates on the frames in
case you might get the century wrong not believing it
could be you till they put you out in the rain at closing-time

B: no sight of the face or any other part never turned to her nor
she to you always parallel like on an axle-tree never turned
to each other just blurs on the fringes of the field no
touching or anything of that nature always space between if
only an inch no pawing in the manner of flesh and blood no
better than shades no worse if it wasn't for the vows

A: no getting out to it that way so what next no question of asking not another word to the living as long as you lived so foot it up in the end to the station bowed half double get out to it that way all closed down and boarded up Doric terminus of the Great Southern and Eastern all closed down and the colonnade crumbling away so what next

C: the rain and the old rounds trying making it up that way as you went along how it would work that way for a change never having been how never having been would work the old rounds trying to wangle you into it tottering and muttering all over the parish till the words dried up and the head dried up and the legs dried up whosever they were or it gave up whoever it was

B: stock still always stock still like that time on the stone or that time in the sand stretched out parallel in the sand in the sun gazing up at the blue or eyes closed blue dark blue dark stock still side by side scene float up and there you were wherever it was

A: gave it up gave up and sat down on the steps in the pale morning sun no those steps got no sun somewhere else then gave up and off somewhere else and down on a step in the pale sun a doorstep say someone's doorstep for it to be time to get on the night ferry and out to hell out of there no need sleep anywhere not a curse for the old scenes the old names the passers pausing to gape at you quick gape then pass pass on pass by on the other side

B: stock still side by side in the sun then sink and vanish without your having stirred any more than the two knobs on a dumbbell except the lids and every now and then the lips to vow and all around too all still all sides wherever it might be no stir or sound only faintly the leaves in the little wood behind or the ears or the bent or the reeds as the case might be of man no sight of man or beast no sight or sound

C: always winter then always raining always slipping in

somewhere when no one would be looking in off the street
out of the cold and rain in the old green holeproof coat
your father left you places you hadn't to pay to get in like
the Public Library that was another great thing free culture
far from home or the Post Office that was another another
place another time

A: huddled on the doorstep in the old green greatcoat in the
pale sun with the nightbag needless on your knees not
knowing where you were little by little not knowing where
you were or when you were or what for place might have been
uninhabited for all you knew like that time on the stone the
child on the stone where none ever came
(*Silence 10 seconds. Breath audible. After 3 seconds eyes open.*)

B: or alone in the same the same scenes making it up that way
to keep it going keep it out on the stone (*eyes close*) alone on
the end of the stone with the wheat and blue or the towpath
alone on the towpath with the ghosts of the mules the
drowned rat or bird or whatever it was floating off into the
sunset till you could see it no more nothing stirring only the
water and the sun going down till it went down and you
vanished all vanished

A: none ever came but the child on the stone among the giant
nettles with the light coming in where the wall had
crumbled away poring on his book well on into the night
some moods the moonlight and they all out on the roads
looking for him or making up talk breaking up two or more
talking to himself being together that way where none ever
came

C: always winter then endless winter year after year as if it
couldn't end the old year never end like time could go no
further that time in the Post Office all bustle Christmas
bustle in off the street when no one was looking out of the
cold and rain pushed open the door like anyone else and
straight for the table neither right nor left with all the forms
and the pens on their chains sat down first vacant seat and
were taking a look round for a change before drowsing away

14

B: or that time alone on your back in the sand and no vows to break the peace when was that an earlier time a later time before she came after she went or both before she came after she was gone and you back in the old scene wherever it might be might have been the same old scene before as then then as after with the rat or the wheat the yellowing ears or that time in the sand the glider passing over that time you went back soon after long after

A: eleven or twelve in the ruin on the flat stone among the nettles in the dark or moonlight muttering away now one voice now another there was childhood for you till there on the step in the pale sun you heard yourself at it again not a curse for the passers pausing to gape at the scandal huddled there in the sun where it had no warrant clutching the nightbag drooling away out loud eyes closed and the white hair pouring out down from under the hat and so sat on in that pale sun forgetting it all

C: perhaps fear of ejection having clearly no warrant in the place to say nothing of the loathsome appearance so this look round for once at your fellow bastards thanking God for once bad and all as you were you were not as they till it dawned that for all the loathing you were getting you might as well not have been there at all the eyes passing over you and through you like so much thin air was that the time or was that another time another place another time

B: the glider passing over never any change same blue skies nothing ever changed but she with you there or not on your right hand always the right hand on the fringe of the field and every now and then in the great peace like a whisper so faint she loved you hard to believe you even you made up that bit till the time came in the end

A: making it all up on the doorstep as you went along making yourself all up again for the millionth time forgetting it all where you were and what for Foley's Folly and the lot the child's ruin you came to look was it still there to hide in again till it was night and time to go till that time came

C: the Library that was another another place another time that
    time you slipped in off the street out of the cold and rain
    when no one was looking what was it then you were never
    the same after never again after something to do with dust
    something the dust said sitting at the big round table with a
    bevy of old ones poring on the page and not a sound

B: that time in the end when you tried and couldn't by the
    window in the dark and the owl flown to hoot at someone
    else or back with a shrew to its hollow tree and not another
    sound hour after hour hour after hour not a sound when
    you tried and tried and couldn't any more no words left to
    keep it out so gave it up gave up there by the window in the
    dark or moonlight gave up for good and let it in and nothing
    the worse a great shroud billowing in all over you on top of
    you and little or nothing the worse little or nothing

A: back down to the wharf with the nightbag and the old green
    greatcoat your father left you trailing the ground and the
    white hair pouring out down from under the hat till that
    time came on down neither right nor left not a curse for the
    old scenes the old names not a thought in your head only
    get back on board and away to hell out of it and never
    come back or was that another time all that another time
    was there ever any other time but that time away to hell out
    of it all and never come back

C: not a sound only the old breath and the leaves turning and
    then suddenly this dust whole place suddenly full of dust
    when you opened your eyes from floor to ceiling nothing
    only dust and not a sound only what was it it said come
    and gone was that it something like that come and gone
    come and gone no one come and gone in no time gone in no
    time

    (*Silence 10 seconds. Breath audible. After 3 seconds eyes open.
    After 5 seconds smile, toothless for preference. Hold 5 seconds
    till fade out and curtain.*)